KEEP YOUR VISION ALIVE

~

ABRAHAM M. SIAFA

JB TREMONT, LLC
Delaware

Published by JB Tremont, LLC
P.O. Box 301, Glenside, Pennsylvania, 19038, U.S.A.

Copyright © by Abraham M. Siafa, 2014

ISBN 13: 978-0-692-31128-8
ISBN 10: 0-692-31128-9

Printed in the United States of America

Cover design by James Berry, Getyourwebpage.com

All Rights Reserved

www.jbtremont.com

DEDICATION

I would like to dedicate "Keep Your Vision Alive" to all Springs of Joy members around the world. To my friends who challenged, inspired, encouraged and prayed for me along the way. You mean so much to me and you are so special. To my two beautiful daughters, Praise and Precious: you are the best in the world. I am sure I could not have made it without you giving me a reason to go on. Thank you for giving me the gift of having you in my life.

INTRODUCTION

You can have the life you have always imagined. You can live your God-given dreams. Even when the going gets tough, you can keep moving forward. Your setbacks can be turned into comebacks. For you to succeed, three main things are required:

A Clear Vision

A Winning Attitude

The Right Relationships

This book, "Keep Your Vision Alive," is not just a book, it is a battle plan.

This book is here to equip and empower you to accomplish everything that God has put into your heart.

I have devoted my life to sharing what I have learnt and have helped people get to the next level. Life has become meaningless to many, because they do not have a vision. Everyone is looking for a better way to be successful. It is to this end that this book comes to help you realize your dream. I intend to share with every reader the blue print to keeping your vision alive.

So Get Ready, For You Are On Your Way To Making It Happen In Any Area Of Your Life!

TABLE OF CONTENTS

CHAPTER ONE
UNDERSTANDING VISION

"The most pathetic person in the world is someone who has sight but no vision." – Helen Keller

In order to keep your vision alive, you must first: have a vision and a firm understanding of it. Having a vision is not enough; it must be combined with determination, faith, hope and passion. God created man to fulfill a purpose. No one was created or born to fail, so then one can ask the big question.

WHAT IS VISION?

o Vision Is The Art Of Seeing What Is Invisible To Others.

o Vision Is The Capacity To Believe In What Others Cannot See, But You See It, Believe And Prepare For It.

o Vision Is What You See, To Accomplish What You Desire, To Get What You Want.

o Vision Is Like A Design Or Plan Of A Finished Product That You Are About To Produce.

o Vision Is A Mental Picture Of A Future State.

o Vision Is The Vehicle That Transports You Into Your God-Given Destiny.

o Vision Is A Picture Of Where You Want To End Up.

o Vision Is A Mental Picture Of What The Future Holds.

o Vision Is Today Pregnant With Tomorrow.

o Vision Is The Catalyst For Success. It Is An Idea Inspired By God.

o Vision Is A Project That You See In Your Heart.

You will never be celebrated until you are a vision-carrier. Only those who can see the invisible will do the impossible.

The most valuable people in the world are visionary people. To be without a vision is to be without a purpose. In other words, to be without a vision is to be purposeless.

The Bible states, *"Where there is no vision, the people perish." (Proverbs*

4

29:18, KJV). Vision is not a vague wish or dream or hope. It is a picture of real results, of real efforts. It gives you a specific direction. Without vision, you have no direction. If you do not know where you are going, you may probably end up somewhere else…

Abraham M. Siafa

6

CHAPTER TWO
NEED AND IMPORTANCE OF VISION

Where there is no vision the people perish.

Proverbs 29:18 (KJV)

Vision is absolutely necessary and important for advancement in life and purpose. In other words, where there is vision there is life. Everyone needs a vision, because it determines ones future. What you see is what you get.

Vision will open doors beyond measure and gives you a bold reason for living. Life cannot be improved without vision, because it is necessary for progress.

Vision will determine your destiny and marks you out for distinction. It also helps you to achieve your goals faster. When you do not have a vision or a plan for the future, your mind has no choice but to dwell in the past. Not everyone who dreams wins, but all winners are dreamers. Those who look behind will never see beyond.

In Chapter One, we started by saying everyone created by God was created to fulfill a purpose and no one was born to fail. Simply put, you are on a mission on planet earth.

To be a success in your mission or on any of life's endeavors, you need to have a vision and a firm understanding of it, because it is what gives you the specific direction to follow in order to accomplish it. The following points can further explain the need and importance of vision.

1. Vision Helps You to Be A Better Leader

Vision activates people. It puts them to work; it gives them something to do.

The work of a visionary is to get your INSIDE VISION to manifest OUTSIDE. People will follow someone as a leader who has a vision and purpose. A visionary has the ability and capability to carry others along towards the fulfillment of that vision. Every successful business, ministry, institution or organization is a result of a visionary leader.

2. Vision Brings Opposition

Every vision comes with opposition.

Everyone will not believe in you or your dream. Even family members, close friends, etc. can sometimes be your opposition. Some will love you and some will hate you, because of your vision. Your success in any level creates opportunity for envy. The size of your vision determines the level of attacks.

Having a vision does not mean everything will go smoothly. You will have to face opposition, various obstacles, setbacks and barriers. Being focused on your vision in the midst of these will help you triumph. Your opposition can also be your opportunity depending on how you see it.

3. Vision Brings Provision

Every God-ordained vision comes with provision. If He sends you, He will pay the bills. If you send yourself, you will pay the bill. **God is too purposeful to fail.**

God gives provision proportionate to the vision He gave to you. He gives you a vision, and wisdom to attract the resources you need to complete your mission. He always backs you and will never allow you to fail, because of His resources. He has already made the provision before He sent you on the mission.

12

CHAPTER THREE
UNDERSTANDING PURPOSE

*Vision and purpose are
always connected.*

Purpose is the ultimate reason for the creation of a thing – it is the <u>why</u> of a thing. God does nothing without purpose. God is a God of purpose.

Nothing in life is without a purpose. Purpose creates the mission and produces the vision. The discovery of purpose will bring meaning to your life.

Purpose is the pre-knowledge of where you are going. To succeed in life is to know what you are called to do and be purpose-driven until you get there. So many people die with unborn dreams and aspirations, because they have not known their purpose or why they are here, focused on it, and/or labored to make it a reality.

Purpose is to life what a rudder is to a ship or a steering wheel is to a car. It is the resoluteness of your mind.

A man of purpose is a man of impact. When you are living on purpose, you do not waste your time, but maximize it. The difference between achievers and failures are what they do with their time. Time has power to dictate our destiny. Time lost cannot be recovered. Time wasters are destiny killers.

To know and live your purpose is to maximize your potential. You were created with a special gift, a talent and potential that God equipped you with to fulfill your destiny. All you need to do

15

is to identify it and use it to the best of your ability.

To know your purpose and pursue it is to avoid the wrong environment and people. Your environment and association will determine if, or what you will manifest. The right product in the wrong location will not yield profit.

The people and environment you connect with will either make or break you. If those around you think below you, then you are limited, because you are surrounded with mediocrity. Sometimes you have to make a hard decision to move ahead, which can sometimes hurt your friends, relatives – the people you love.

Your decision to move ahead may sometimes challenge others to think about their own lives. You need people who think like you, above you and challenge your potential.

CHAPTER FOUR
THE MENTOR, THE
COLLEAGUE, AND THE
PROTEGE

God Has Put People In Your Life For A Reason And For A Season. It Is Very Important To Know The Reason And The Season You Are In When Running With Your Vision.

There are three (3) types of people who will cross your path whom God wants to use to accomplish His purpose in your life or use you to make a difference or impact in their lives.

1. <u>MENTOR</u>

> *Mentoring is a partnership that exists between two (2) people (mentor and mentee) in a similar field or similar experiences.*

A mentor is an individual who is dependable, trustworthy, effective, engaged and authentic in what the mentee is looking for. He can be seen as your future. One who has gone ahead of you, gotten what you want, or achieved what you want to achieve. A mentor is where you want to be.

A mentor can help you realize your dream faster. Through counsel and godly advice, a mentor will help you <u>not</u> to make deadly mistakes. He is one who guides you, because he is more experienced and can also be seen as a role model.

A mentor is someone whom you listen to, whose advice, direction, guidance, and opinion you follow. Mentoring is absolutely necessary to keeping your vision alive. There are certain **key factors** you need to look at when choosing your mentor:

   a. An individual with up-to-date knowledge and experience on your subject.

b. Shares similar values and leads by example.

c. Willing to share expertise, skills, and knowledge, and has good mentoring and management skills.

d. Has integrity and leads by example.

e. Has good contacts or networks, and creates opportunities, open doors and wants you to succeed.

f. Knows your strengths, abilities, and weaknesses, and is reliable.

g. Wants you to succeed, be independent and desires to help others succeed.

h. Ready to devote his time and energy into the mentoring process.

The Bible states:

> *Where there is no counsel the people fall, but in the multitude of counselors there is safety.*
>
> *Proverbs 11:14 (NKJV)*

To keep your vision alive and accomplish it, you need to have a mentor. You cannot succeed without listening to others. A mentor will not always be an old person. While it is assumed an older person may impart wisdom, a younger person can have a deeper understanding or insight on a subject, as well as, an unexpected perspective

2. <u>COLLEAGUE</u>

A colleague can be a fellow worker, an associate, a member of your staff or fellow professional.

Your colleagues can be seen as where you are now – your present. They are people on your same level. They can be close friends or even family members. Some colleagues have similar traits as you, like sense of humor, respect, responsibility, etc.

The difference between a mentor and a colleague is the understanding and insight they have about what you are looking for. Therefore, you should be watchful not to make the mistake of regarding a colleague as a mentor. For if you do, you will be limited and will not rise above mediocrity, because you are on the same level. A colleague may lack the experience, expertise, skill, etc. that you need to get to the next level.

Your colleagues may be ahead of you, because of one reason or another, but that does not make them your mentor. They should help you hate mediocrity and challenge you to be better at what you are doing.

3. PROTÉGÉ

A protégé is defined as one who gets help or has been promoted by someone in his field.

A protégé is your past. That is, where you used to be. They believe in you, submit to you and follow your guidance. He or she is a person who crosses your path to feed from you and sees you as a mentor.

Every mentor may have once been a protégé. He has gone through his experience and is now in a better place to help the protégé navigate through and become a better person.

God does not want us to be receivers alone, but to be givers as well. You are blessed to be a blessing. Therefore, as a

26

mentor, you take time to invest in the life of a protégé.

A protégé goes to a mentor because they see their future in the mentor, and they want to be a part of something that is greater or bigger than themselves. As a mentor, you invest in a protégé, because you want to have a lasting legacy.

***

Understanding where you are and who you are in your journey to keeping your vision alive and accomplishing it is very crucial. There are times when a colleague will want to be a mentor in your life or a protégé feels he or she has arrived and does not need your mentorship. There are also times when mentors are jealous of a protégé's fast-paced or quick success. BEWARE. **You should know the role you are playing, at a particular time, in the life of anyone.**

CHAPTER FIVE
LESSONS FROM THE EAGLE

Dr. Myles Monroe shares principles of an Eagle.[1] As a leader, you can apply these principles and learn valuable lessons from them. These lessons will help you soar above every storm, jump over every obstacle, and break through any barrier you are facing as you move towards keeping your vision alive.

1. Clear Vision

Eagles have a clear, fine and strong vision. They have the ability to focus on something up to five (5) kilometers

---

[1] Hetri, Ian D. "The 6 Positive Leadership Traits of Eagle Man Should Learn From." HubPages, Inc. 2012. Web. <http://iandabasorihetr.hubpages.com/hub/7-Leadership-Characteristics-of-An-Eagle-That-Man-Should-Learn-From>.

away, which far exceeds the vision of most birds. When an Eagle sees his prey, he narrows his focus on it and sets out to get it. No matter the obstacles, the Eagle will not move his focus from the prey until he grabs it. **Great leaders, like Eagles are visionaries – they are able to see far beyond what others may see, focus on it and grab it.**

2. Fearless

An Eagle never surrenders to the size or strength of its prey or attacker. It gives a fight to win or regain its territory. **Great leaders are fearless.**

3. Tenacious

When other birds fly away from a storm with fear, the Eagle spreads its mighty wings and uses the current to soar to greater heights. The Eagle takes advantage of the very storm that the lesser birds fear and from which they run for cover. Eagles glide with the current of the storm. A visionary or leader can rise to greater heights if s/he takes the challenges head on without running away from them. **A great leader solves a problem, even in the midst of a storm.**

4. High Flyers

Eagles can fly up to an altitude of 10,000 feet and still are able to swiftly land on the ground. At that altitude, you will never find another bird, only Eagles.

Eagles do not mingle with pigeons. Pigeons scavenge on the ground. They grumble and complain all day long, while Eagles do not. Eagles fly and make less noise, waiting for an opportunity to strike their next prey. Although great leaders are visionary and fly high, they must possess the ability to quickly land on their feet. In other words, **Great leaders must be grounded, relatable, and down-to-earth.**

5. Possess Vitality

Eagles are full of life, energy and vitality. They never give up living. They re-energize themselves. There is a certain time in the life of an Eagle, when it must make hard choices – re-energize, or die. The Eagle retreats to the top of the mountain to go through a period of transformation. It knocks off its beak, plucks off its talons and plucks out its feathers. Each stage produces regrowth of the removed parts allowing the Eagle to live another 30 to 40 years. **Great leaders also make hard choices, and must go through periods of personal development and transformation.**

6. Never Eat Dead Things

Eagles never eat dead or lifeless things. They never eat meat that they have not killed; they are not scavengers. They feed only on fresh prey. Vultures eat dead animals, but Eagles do not.

Great leaders should not feed on old, dead things. Be careful what you feed your eyes, your mind, your heart, your spirit. Be certain your information is not outdated, old-fashioned, or stuck in the past. Always be up to date with information and do your research well.

CHAPTER SIX
OBSTACLES TO KEEPING
YOUR VISION ALIVE

A visionary is always faced with various obstacles and challenges. As stated in Chapter Two, having a vision does not mean you will have smooth sailing in life. These challenges and obstacles are meant to deter or stop you, but you can use them as a stepping stone to your next level. The following are some obstacles you are likely to face:

1. Fear

Fear is believing that what you cannot see will come to pass. Someone defined fear as False Evidence Appearing Real.

It is a state of the mind. It can stop you from doing what you want to do. It can age you, paralyze you, and kill your dream.

Fear limits your vision and kills your self-esteem. If you are not living your dream, then you are living your fear. If you are not walking by faith then you are walking by fear.

So many times we are afraid of our past, afraid of making mistakes, afraid that everyone will not like us or afraid of not succeeding. Despite these facts, we can also do something to get rid of fear.

HOW TO GET RID OF FEAR

a. Guard your mind against negative news, people, conversations and environments. Turn a deaf ear to the things that contribute to your fear.

b. Listen to the things that empower you to create a new reality for yourself.

c. Write your ideas down and take the lead.

d. Change the way you see yourself. Stop beating yourself up because of a mistake you have made. Have a healthy self-image about yourself.

e. Change your focus and daily routine. Your life becomes what you do every day. Focus on the right things.

f. Always have the "It's possible" mentality.

g. Do not run from your fears, but face them head on again and again and conquer them.

h. Fear is controlled by the questions you ask. If you ask different questions you will get different answers. Always ask questions on how it can be better and you will get answers in that area.

i. Lastly, there is what is called the "I can" factor. To get rid of fear, always confess what you can and what you are. It builds your confidence and self-esteem.

2. Lack of Finance

Vision has the ability to attract or pull the required resources. Lack of finance should not stop you from keeping your vision alive, but should motivate you to step up, stay focused and do something about it. It is very easy to abort your dream or allow it to die because of finance, but being steady and focused will bring ideas on how you can get what you want.

3. Prophets of Doom

There are people who can be called prophets of doom. They are people who have already programmed your failure and will give you 100 reasons why you cannot and why it is not going to happen. Most of the time, they do this because they cannot accomplish anything in life or they see you as a threat to what they are doing.

Prophets of doom will try to make fear grip your heart so that you can stay in your cocoon. Their aim is to intimidate you, so that you will lose your self-esteem and eventually lose your dream. DO NOT LISTEN TO THEM! Listen to your heart.

Do not be intimidated! You do not have a spirit of fear, but you have a spirit of power, love and a sound mind. (2 Timothy 1:7) Move away from prophets of doom and keep them far from you. Do not give them access to your dream.

CHAPTER SEVEN
HOW TO KEEP YOUR VISION ALIVE

In the previous chapters we have looked at the meaning of vision and obstacles encountered when keeping your vision alive. This chapter focuses on what you can do to sustain your vision.

Life is full of challenges, problems and storms. Having a vision will not prevent you from facing the storms, but a proper focus and knowing the direction you are heading will help you accomplish your vision. Life's storms come for a reason and for a season. Discover what you can learn through a storm and navigate your way through it. Do not let a storm stop you from moving forward.

<u>Steps to Keeping Your Vision Alive:</u>

1. Write Down the Vision

Write down the vision and make it plain...
Habakkuk 2:2

Do not just pray about it, think about it or plan in your mind, but write your vision down.

Writing it down helps you to:

a. Visualize
b. Set goals and objectives
c. Clearly define your goals
d. Develop a plan and work the plan. This is the first step to keeping your vision alive.

44

2. Enlarge Your Vision

Do not just have a vision but enlarge your vision.

You have to conceive it on the inside before you receive it on the outside. The barrier is in your mind. **Always see the bigger picture.** The image has to be part of your conversation, deep down in your subconscious mind, in your actions and in every part of your being. What you see is what you get.

If your vision is small in the inside, you will make a small impact and vice versa. Donald Trump has said, "I like thinking big; if you're going to be thinking anything, you might as well think big." A big or enlarged vision results in big pursuits and big accomplishments. Someone once said, "If your dream is not big enough, it won't move the hearts of men".

So always enlarge you vision and dream big.

3. Focus

Being focused in keeping your vision alive is to pay attention to it despite the obstacles, distractions and challenges.

A lot of things are bound to come your way which will tend to take you off your path, but you should be determined to keep the main thing the main thing or remain focused.

You are here to make it your own unique contribution to the world. Always focus the future. **Focus gives**

46

you a road map to reach your destination. Focus helps you to stay on course so that nothing will blow you off.

4. Work Hard and Smart

It is advised to work smart, but you also need to put much effort or hard work into what you are doing.

No one is going to make your dream come true but you. Having a vision without working hard to bring it to pass is just fantasy. You should always set goals and objectives.

Goals show you were you are now and where you are heading. Goals help you to put in extra effort, extra work, because you know what is expected of you. They provide direction, a sense of

47

purpose and motivate others to work harder.

Between your goals and accomplishments is discipline and hard work. **You have to work your vision.** Be a part of something that is bigger than you. Put effort into what you do and don't just talk about it. Do it and let the fruit of your actions speak.

5. Say Goodbye

Anything you want to do starts with a decision. You can never reach your destination without leaving your departure point. You cannot be all things to all people. Be different and unique.

Keeping your vision alive requires saying goodbye to anything that is

standing in your way. Anything Means Anything. It is a hard decision, but absolutely necessary.

Vision carriers are not afraid of loneliness, because it is lonely at the top. You know what is burning inside of you and what you are pregnant with. Only you know the pains you are going through to birth your vision; no one else knows your pain. So be ready to make the hard decisions, choices and push until something happens.

6. Positive Mindset

> *As a man thinketh in his heart so is he.*
>
> *Proverbs 23:7(KJV)*

Always be positive about your vision no matter what you see, feel or hear.

A positive mindset will:

a. Attract positive things
b. Boost your motivation
c. Reduce stress
d. Help you make better decision during pressure
e. Help you to identify solutions
f. Keep you healthy

You are a product of your thoughts. Negative thoughts breed negativity, whilst positive thought breeds positivity. **Your thoughts are directly related to your actions.**

Thoughts become reality, so guard your thoughts, because you easily become what you think. **Always see yourself where you want to be and not where**

you are now. This will help you get through difficult times and storms.

7. Depend On God

> *It's not him that willeth or him that doeth, but God that showeth mercy.*
>
> *Romans 9:16*

One of the most important steps to keeping your vision alive is depending on God, because He gave you the vision. So no matter your efforts, it is Him who gives the increase. Always see God as your source and cling to Him.

8. Let Go of The Past

> *We can be prisoners of our past if we do not let go.*

Letting go of our past is very crucial. You may have good reasons for feeling the way you do. You may have gone through things you did not deserve to go through. You may have been abused verbally, physically, emotionally, sexually or maybe someone took advantage of you. Let it go...

God has a reason why He allowed you to go through what you went through. All things will eventually work out for your good. Your past should make you better, wiser and should not be your breaking point. It should always be seen as a testimony of God's goodness and mercy.

Your past cannot determine your destiny. Let it go and focus on your future, which is brighter and better. Whenever thoughts of your past come, always overcome them with thoughts of a bigger, brighter and better future. **Do not allow your past to kill your vision or keep you from fulfilling your destiny.**

9. Find Strength through Adversity

Use your adversity as a challenge and opportunity to take you to the next level.

We all face adversity in life, but the truth is what you do in and through your adversity. **Do not ever back down!** Although your adversity is meant to destroy you, use it to your advantage.

Adversity is part of life. It depends on how you see it and interpret it. One man's problem can be another man's miracle or breakthrough. Remember to always ask God what you can learn from adversity and ask for His grace to sail through that period of your life.

CHAPTER EIGHT
POSTIVE QUOTES ON VISION
AND LEADERSHIP

Compiled below are fifty (50) quotes from various visionaries and leaders that will help you on your journey. These quotes are meant to motivate, inspire, and encourage you to keep your vision alive.

1. In order to carry a positive action, we must develop a positive vision

   – Dalai Lama

2. Leadership is the capacity to translate vision into reality

   – Warren Bennis

3. Vision without action is merely a dream. Action without vision just passes time. Vision with action can change the world.

> – Joel A. Barker

4. Where there is no vision there is no hope.

> – George Washington Carver

5. The vision must be followed by the venture. It is not enough to stare up the steps. We must step up the stairs.

> – Vance Havner

6. Your vision will become clear only when you look into your own heart.

Who looks outside dreams, who looks inside awakes.

– Carl Jung

7. Leaders establish the vision for the future and set the strategy for getting there.

– John P. Kotter

8. Just because a man lacks the use of his eyes doesn't mean he lacks vision.

– Stevie Wonder

9. When you have vision it affects your attitude. Your attitude is optimistic rather than pessimistic

– Unknown

10. Capital isn't scary; vision is.

         – Sam Walton

11. It is a terrible thing to see and have no vision.

         – Helen Keller

12. When I think of vision I have in mind the ability to see beyond the majority.

         – Charles R. Swindoll

13. Create a compelling vision, one that takes people to a new place and then translate that vision into reality.

         – Warren Bennis

14. It takes vision and courage to create. It takes faith and courage to prove.

    – Owen D. Young

15. Not many people will give you a vision of what the future will bring you.

    – Will. I. AM

16. The vision that you glorify in your mind, the idea that you enthrone in your heart, this you will build your life by and this you will become.

    – Unknown

17. Without vision even the most focused passion is a battery without a device.

– Ken Auletta

18. Leadership is about vision and responsibility, not power.

– Seth Berkley

19. A vision is not just a picture of what you could do, it is an appeal to our better selves, a call to become something more.

– Rosabeth Moss Kanter

20. Leaders need to be optimists. Their vision is beyond the present.

– Rudy Giuliani

21. It is important to be true to yourself and to your vision.

– Nicole Polizzi

22. You've got to have a vision. You've got to have a message.

– Scott Walker

23. Anyone who limits her vision to memories of yesterday is already dead.

– Lillie Langtry

24. If you have a vision, do something with it.

> – Anthony J. D'Angelo

25. Every age needs men who will redeem the time by living with a vision of things that are to be.

> – Adlai E. Stevenson

26. A director without a vision is a catastrophe.

> – Alan Arkin

27. Vision looks inward and becomes duty.

> – Stephen Samuel Wise

28. The empires of the future are empires of the mind.

    – Winston Churchill

29. A leader has the vision and conviction that a dream can be achieved. He inspires the power and energy to get it done.

    – Ralph Lauren

30. Destiny is not a matter of chance, but of choice. Not something to wish for, but to attain.

    – William Jennings Bryan

31. Big thinking precedes great achievement.

    – Wilferd Peterson

32. Dissatisfaction and discouragement are not caused by the absence of things but the absence of vision.

– Unknown

33. The future belongs to those who see possibilities before they become obvious.

– John Sculley

34. If you limit your choices only to what seems possible or reasonable, you disconnect yourself from what you truly want and all that is left is a compromise.

– Robert Fritz

35. Create your future from your future, not from your past.

    – Werner Erhard

36. Keep your eyes on the stars and your feet on the ground.

    – Franklin D. Roosevelt

37. No matter how dark things seem to be or actually are, raise your sights and see the possibilities. Always see them, for they are always there.

    – Norman Vincent Peale

38. You cannot depend on your eyes when your imagination is out of focus.

    – Mark Twain

39. You've got to think big things while you are doing small things so that the small things will go in the right directions.

　　　　　　　　　　– Alvin Toffler

40. The future belongs to those who see possibilities before they become obvious.

　　　　　　　　　　– John Sculley

41. Leadership is the capacity to translate vision into reality.

　　　　　　　　　　– Warren Bennis

42. Where you come from is not as important as where you are going.

　　　　　　　　　　– Unknown

43. Dreams are extremely important; you can't do it unless you can imagine it.

> – George Lucas

44. Pain pushes until vision pulls

> – Michael Beckwith

45. It's not what the vision is, it's what the vision does.

> – Peter Senge

46. The best vision is insight.

> – Malcolm Forbes

47. I have seen farther than others because I was standing on the shoulders of giants.

    – Isaac Newton

48. If you can dream it, you can do it.

    – Walt Disney

49. He who looks through an open window sees fewer things than he who looks through a closed window.

    – Charles Baudelaire

50. The more boundless your vision is the more real you are.

    – Deepak Chopra.

CONCLUSION

To be or become someone or something, you must first see it before you can become it. The mind is a powerful tool that has been given to mankind.

See your tomorrow today. You are pregnant with a vision that is waiting to be manifested. Do not let it die. Keep it alive.

This book, "Keep Your Vision Alive," is written to inspire you, to aspire and awaken that sleeping giant in you. You have all it takes to get to the next level. You are here for a purpose and have a contribution to make on the planet earth.

You can always be what you desire to be if you have a vision, understand it and run with it, despite the odds and obstacles. Visionaries rule the world. Your vision will distinguish you, take you to places and bring you before great men. Everything you need is in you. Your vision can pull the resources, open the doors and create the opportunities you need. KEEP IT ALIVE.

When you do not have a vision, you do not have a future. When you have one you need to go through the labor of keeping it alive.

Keep Your Vision Alive!!!

www.ingramcontent.com/pod-product-compliance
Lightning Source LLC
LaVergne TN
LVHW051155080426
835508LV00021B/2644